January 2009

Dear Cris,
    May you always find happiness!
Wishing you the best.

        With love,
        Cindy

WORDS TO HELP YOU

BE

HAPPY

IN ALL THE WAYS
THAT MATTER MOST

Other Titles in This Series:

Words to Help You
Be a Success

Words to Help You
Be Positive Every Day

Words to Help You Be Strong
Along the Path of Life

We wish to thank Susan Polis Schutz for permission to reprint the following poems that appear in this publication: "Find Happiness in Everything You Do." Copyright © 1983 by Stephen Schutz and Susan Polis Schutz. And for "Where are all the people...." Copyright © 1979 by Continental Publications. All rights reserved.

Library of Congress Control Number: 2008928820
ISBN: 978-1-59842-254-2

▉ and Blue Mountain Press are registered in U.S. Patent and Trademark Office. Certain trademarks are used under license.

Acknowledgments appear on page 72.

Printed in China.
First Printing: 2008

♻ This book is printed on recycled paper.

This book is printed on fine quality, laid embossed, 80 lb. paper. This paper has been specially produced to be acid free (neutral pH) and contains no groundwood or unbleached pulp. It conforms with the requirements of the American National Standards Institute, Inc., so as to ensure that this book will last and be enjoyed by future generations.

Blue Mountain Arts, Inc.
P.O. Box 4549, Boulder, Colorado 80306

WORDS TO HELP YOU

BE
HAPPY
IN ALL THE WAYS
THAT MATTER MOST

Edited by Gary Morris

Blue Mountain Press™
Boulder, Colorado

$\mathcal{H}$appiness is… the pure, unselfish gift of life that is found once we appreciate the things in life that mean the most.

— *Barbara J. Hall*

Introduction

$\mathcal{W}$ise words are such wonderful things. Just a few perfect words, spoken or shared at the right time, can change our lives. They can keep us healthy and safe and strong. They can guide us and inspire us. They can teach us how to travel life's path in the best possible way... and avoid some of the problems and pitfalls. They can give us courage. They can give us faith.

Within the pages of this book, you will discover some of the most encouraging and insightful advice you've ever heard. You will be introduced to a number of things you've never read before — but that you'll never forget for as long as you live.

These pearls of wisdom come from a wide variety of remarkable people who share a common message. They believe in being happy, in choosing wisely, and in making each day as rewarding as it can possibly be.

Listen to their conversation, take their messages to heart, and let their words help you be happy... as you continue on your journey through life.

— *Douglas Pagels*

If You Want to Be Happy...

*B*elieve in yourself and all you want to be. Don't let what other people say or do make you frown. Laugh as much as possible. Let in the good times and get through the bad. Be happy with who and where you are. You are in the right place, and your heart is leading you on the way to a great tomorrow. When circumstances seem difficult, pull through them. This will make you stronger than you think. The longer you practice the habit of working toward your dreams, the easier the journey will become. You were meant for great things. Learn as much as possible. Always follow your dreams.

— *Ashley Rice*

Ten Golden Rules...

1. Live your life with purpose; don't just do "whatever," or "whatever" might just be what you get.

2. Develop a compassionate spirit and a loving heart; you will feel better about yourself, and others will feel better about you.

3. Be honest and guard your integrity no matter what the rest of the world is doing; they're not the ones who have to live with you — you are.

4. Believe in yourself and always do what's right; a clear conscience will keep you on the right path.

5. Be as good as your word and don't make promises you're not going to keep.

...for a Happy Life

6. Be fair to others, especially those less fortunate; there may come a time you have to walk in their shoes.

7. Keep a positive attitude and speak encouraging words; you'll hear them rise up in you when you need them, and others will remember them when they need lifting up.

8. Don't take your natural talents for granted; use them to nourish your soul and to touch lives, and they will be multiplied.

9. When you feel discouraged or unlucky, remember the times you've been fortunate, and that knowledge will help balance out your fears.

10. Remember that what you do today will show up tomorrow, so when you make important decisions, think about tomorrow today.

— *Donna Fargo*

The World's a Brighter Place...

A happy person is not someone to whom "bad" things do not happen, or who ignores the negative in some kind of forced reverie that more resembles Pollyanna than anything real or human. Rather, it is someone who understands that his or her *reaction* to events — not the external conditions that are subject to the vagaries of many conflicting forces, most of which are out of our control — are the stuff of happiness.

— *Alan Epstein, PhD*

...Because of Happy People

Happy people are accepting of themselves, so they don't spend precious time in regret. They accept others, too, so are free to love people as they are, rather than expending energy trying to do a repair job on everyone in sight. They look positively to the future so they don't spend a lot of time in worry or fear. They are engaged with life as a wonderful adventure in which they are here to give their best. The zest with which they encounter life is contagious; people are drawn into their orbit and success seems to be attracted as well. They're healthier, too.

— *M. J. Ryan*

*H*appy people have the ability
  to share their lives with others.
They are honest in word and deed,
they are sincere and compassionate,
and they always make sure
that love is a part of everything.
They have the ability
to give to others
and help them with the changes
  that come their way.

Happy people are not afraid
of being vulnerable;
they believe in their uniqueness
    and are proud to be who they are.
They allow themselves the pleasures
of being close to others
    and caring about their happiness.
They have come to understand
that love is what makes
    the difference in life.
They truly make a beautiful difference
    in this world.

— Deanna Beisser

There Is So Much Happiness...

The pathway to happiness is taken step by step. But it is not a path that is touched with the feet. It exists in a realm of true beliefs; a place where the heart helps to lead the way, and the spirit always finds the will to go on.

...to Find Along Your Way

It is so important to take confidence along as your companion and to erase any notions that serve as limitations. You can go beyond the barriers that have halted so many others. You are such a capable, amazing individual. You can strive. You can summon strength you never even knew you possessed.

You can discover
     everything you've always
          imagined you could be.

   You can reach out to new possibilities
        and true happiness.

— *Douglas Pagels*

Start with Joy

There's a reason why the sunrise is so beautiful and magnificent. It sets the stage for a positive, fulfilling day.

When you start the day by choosing to be joyful, you put yourself in a creative, effective state of mind. You'll make yourself better able to handle whatever may come your way during the day.

A relationship that gets off to a positive start at the very beginning will quickly flourish and build great value. You can forge a positive relationship with each day when you begin it in a joyful way.

Even if the day is gray and gloomy you can choose to start it with a positive experience of your own making. Fulfillment comes to those who make it happen, and there's no better time than the beginning of your day to start moving forward.

There's an endless list of ways in which you can begin the day on a positive note. And the days that start well have the best chance of going well.

A new day arrives, ready to be lived. Choose to start it with joy.

— *Ralph Marston*

Your Greatest Asset Is...

*T*o get up each morning with the resolve to be happy... is to set our own conditions to the events of each day. To do this is to condition circumstances instead of being conditioned by them.

— *Ralph Waldo Emerson*

*I*t isn't what you have or who you are or where you are or what you are doing that makes you happy or unhappy. It is what you think about it. For example, two people may be in the same place, doing the same thing; both may have about an equal amount of money and prestige — and yet one may be miserable and the other happy. Why? Because of a different mental attitude.

— *Dale Carnegie*

...an Optimistic Attitude

*H*ow true is it that,
if we are cheerful and contented,
all nature smiles,
the air seems more balmy,
the sky clearer,
the earth has a brighter green...
the flowers are more fragrant...
and the sun, moon, and stars
all appear more beautiful,
and seem to rejoice with us.

— *Orison Swett Marden*

You Can Always Find Something to Be Glad About

Be glad every morning that you've been given a brand-new opportunity to fulfill your hopes and dreams.

Be glad for all the seasons and the beauty they bring to your life: the hopeful springs, the blossoming summers, the brilliant autumns, and the quiet fire of winter days.

Be glad for your talents, whatever they may be; they make you absolutely unique, and they were given so that you could make your own special contribution to this earth.

— *Jon Peyton*

$\mathcal{G}$ratitude is not precisely the same thing as optimism. It's more the attitude that makes optimism possible. It is essentially a habit of thinking, a way of understanding who we are and what happens in our lives. That means, of course, that looking at life through the lens of gratitude is something each of us can do. We can choose gratitude. And here is the fundamental conviction that we must engrave on our hearts if we want the rosy glow of gratitude to light up our lives: Life is a gift, a wonderful, stupendous, miraculous gift. It's not something we deserve or purchase with our efforts. It is simply there for us every morning, waiting for us to unwrap and enjoy. Every moment, in fact, we have the opportunity to open another tiny package in the gift of our days.

— *Thomas Kinkade*

More than a feeling and
deeper than any emotion,

joy

is a pure state of being.

*J*oy is being in love and sleeping in the sunshine and running down a mountain path with the swiftness of a deer in the springtime. Joy expands your heart and opens your soul until you know, really know, that death is simply the turning of another page. Joy is snowflakes and slipping on the ice and getting up so you can slip all over again and never even feeling the cold. Living in joy doesn't mean putting on a happy face. It means that joy is at the core of who you are and always have been. Joy is strong enough to carry you through the darkness and the pain into a place where joy still resides in ultimate measure. Seek to find joy and let joy fill your life.

— *Rachel Snyder*

The Little Roads
to Happiness

The little roads to happiness,
    they are not hard to find;
They do not lead to great success —
    but to a quiet mind.
They do not lead to mighty power,
    nor to substantial wealth.
They bring one to a book, a flower,
    a song of cheer and health.
The little roads to happiness are free
    to everyone;
They lead one to the wind's caress,
    to kiss of friendly sun.

These little roads are shining white,
　　for all the world to see;
Their sign-boards, pointing left and right,
　　are love and sympathy.
The little roads of happiness have this
　　most charming way;
No matter how they may digress
　　throughout the busy day;
No matter where they twist and wind
　　through fields of rich delight,
They're always of the self-same mind
　　to lead us home at night.

　　　　　　　　　— *Wilhelmina Stitch*

For most of life, nothing wonderful happens. If you don't enjoy getting up and working and finishing your work and sitting down to a meal with family or friends, then the chances are that you're not going to be very happy. If someone bases his happiness or unhappiness on major events like a great new job, huge amounts of money, a flawlessly happy marriage or a trip to Paris, that person isn't going to be happy much of the time. If, on the other hand, happiness depends on a good breakfast, flowers in the yard, a drink, or a nap, then we are more likely to live with quite a bit of happiness.

— *Andy Rooney*

$\mathcal{T}$he happiness of life is made up
of minute fractions — the little
soon-forgotten charities of a kiss,
a smile, a kind look, a heartfelt
compliment in the disguise of a
playful raillery, and the countless
other infinitesimals of pleasurable
thought and genial feeling.

— *Samuel Taylor Coleridge*

Fill Your Life
with Everyday Joys

*H*ow little suffices for happiness!... The least thing precisely, the gentlest thing, the lightest thing, a lizard's rustling, a breath, a wink, an eye glance — little maketh up the best happiness. Be still.

— Friedrich Nietzsche

*I*s it so small a thing to have enjoyed the sun, to have lived light in the spring, to have loved, to have thought, to have done?

— Matthew Arnold

*I*t isn't the great big pleasures that count the most; it's making a great deal out of the little ones.

— Jean Webster

$\mathcal{W}$here are all the people
who enjoyed simple things
who used to go out in the sunlight
and sing songs as they gardened
stopping and talking with all the neighbors?
Where are all the people
who enjoyed life
who used to consider the home
the most important place to be
and who used to consider the family
the most important people to be with?
Times have changed most of these people
and urged them to seek the complicated
Yet it is only the very basic simple things
in life
that can make people truly
happy

— *Susan Polis Schutz*

Just for Today...

*Y*ou have a chance to be as happy as any one person has ever been. You have an opportunity to be as proud as anyone you've ever known. You have the potential to make a very special dream come true.

And all you have to do... is recognize the possibilities, the power, and the wonder of... today.

For one remarkable day...

There is a brighter light in your life.
The will to walk up the mountain
takes you exactly where you want
to go. The heart understands what
serenity really means. And your
hopes and wishes and dreams will
not disappear from view.

For one magnificent day...

You can live with an abundance of
love and goodness and grace shining
inside of you. May you make each
day shine... one day at a time.

— *Douglas Pagels*

The Time to Be Happy...

I kept looking for happiness,
and then I realized: This is it.
It's a moment, and it comes,
and it goes, and it'll come back
again. I yearn for things, but at
the same time I'm just peaceful.

— *Nicole Kidman*

*L*earn to enjoy every minute of your life.
Be happy now. Don't wait for something
outside of yourself to make you happy in
the future. Think how precious is the time
you have to spend, whether it's at work or
with your family. Every minute should be
enjoyed and savored.

— *Earl Nightingale*

...Is in This Moment

*W*e do not experience happiness because of what we get. We experience happiness because of how we live each moment.... *Having certain experiences does not make me happy — knowing how to live them with full awareness and to mindfully be in each moment will make me happy.* In this way, happiness is only possible and available in the present moment, and from moment to moment. It comes to us *not* when we are searching for it, for then we are somewhere else other than here and now, but rather when we allow ourselves to be mindful of exactly where we are and fully experience whatever we are doing.

— *Barbara De Angelis, PhD*

How to Be Happy

1. Make up your mind to be happy. Learn to find pleasure in simple things.

2. Make the best of your circumstances. No one has everything, and everyone has something of sorrow intermingled with gladness of life. The trick is to make the laughter outweigh the tears.

3. Don't take yourself too seriously. Don't think that somehow you should be protected from misfortune that befalls other people.

4. You can't please everybody. Don't let criticism worry you.

5. Don't let your neighbor set your standards. Be yourself.

6. Never borrow trouble. Imaginary things are harder to bear than real ones.

7. Do what you can for those less fortunate than yourself.

8. Keep busy at something. A busy person never has time to be unhappy.

— *Robert Louis Stevenson*

Happiness and Work

*H*appiness comes from a job well done, from knowing we've accomplished something of value in a positive and joyous way. Even repetitive, mundane tasks can be made beautiful by the spirit in which we address them. Joy in all we do is something we can choose to cultivate.

The best way to do anything well is to cultivate a love for it.

It makes no sense at all to have our attitudes in conflict with the actions we must take to achieve our goals. That's a sign we need to change what we're doing, change how we feel about it, or both.

Excellence is a function of the attention, care, and concern we give to what we do. Mediocre results from mediocre efforts bring little joy or satisfaction. We can choose to excel and do well through the attention, care, and concern we extend to our work.

Happiness can come from doing an ordinary job extraordinarily well and taking pride in our achievements. Happiness can come from achieving something we value and celebrating our success.

— *Michele Moore*

$\mathcal{T}$he happiest thing that can befall us is to have work given us that requires us to be true to ourselves, and that will count in large benefits to others. There is little pleasure in a daily routine of toil which can be just as well performed by anybody else; but there is abundant happiness in taking up tasks for which we have prepared ourselves, and which would perhaps never be as well done by another. In other words, it is a great privilege to find our own work and get leave to do it.

— *Lucy Larcom*

$\mathcal{F}$ew persons realize how much of their happiness is dependent upon their work, upon the fact that they are kept busy and not left to feed upon themselves. Happiness comes most to persons who seek her least, and think least about it. It is not an object to be sought; it is a state to be induced. It must follow and not lead. It must overtake you, and not you overtake it. How important is health to happiness, yet the best promoter of health is *something to do.*

— *John Burroughs*

$\mathcal{G}$et happiness out of your work or you may never know what happiness is.

— *Elbert Hubbard*

If You Want Fulfillment...

I began learning long ago that those who are happiest are those who do the most for others.

— *Booker T. Washington*

*G*etters generally don't get happiness; givers get it. You simply give to others a bit of yourself — a thoughtful act, a helpful idea, a word of appreciation, a lift over a rough spot, a sense of understanding, a timely suggestion. You take something out of your mind, garnished in kindness out of your heart, and put it into the other fellow's mind and heart.

— *Charles H. Burr*

...Help Others

If you want to be happy, resolutely turn the spotlight off yourself. Forget your own self-importance, your aches and pains, your feelings and fears. Instead, get busy. The world is wide and fascinating, and it needs your participation. People out there need your help. And you need to get off it. A little more service to others, and a little fewer possessions to claim your attention.... Make the world a better place and you make your life worthwhile. Make your life worthwhile and you'll be happy. You don't need to buy anything or ask anybody for advice. You can just go do it.

And you can start right now.

— *Michael Crichton*

*C*heerful people live long in our memory. We remember joy more readily than sorrow, and always look back with tenderness on the brave and cheerful.

— *J. H. Friswell*

*T*here are persons so radiant, so genial, so kind, so pleasure-bearing, that you instinctively feel in their presence that they do you good; whose coming into a room is like bringing a lamp there.

— *Henry Ward Beecher*

*L*et's be grateful for those who give us happiness; they are the charming gardeners who make our souls bloom.

— *Marcel Proust*

*H*ave you ever had your day suddenly turn sunshiny because of a cheerful word? Have you ever wondered if this could be the same world, because someone had been unexpectedly kind to you? You can make today the same for somebody. It is only a question of a little imagination, a little time and trouble. Think now, "What can I do today to make someone happy?"

— *Maltbie D. Babcock*

Share Some
Smiles and Laughter...

Laughter is the sun that drives
winter from the human face.

— *Victor Hugo*

Smile at someone only for the very
important reason that every act of
kindness is another chance to make
this life experience a better one. A
simple smile to someone you've never
met may soften them, and perhaps
the next opportunity they have to
smile at a stranger they will do so,
because they will remember the good
feeling. Try it today.

— *Suzanne Somers*

...and Have Fun

Every once in a while, find some time to run through a sprinkler or two; call up someone you really like and spend an entire day together, even if you do absolutely nothing; work on a project that will probably never enhance your resumé; head for the nearest park and remember what it's like to go down the slide or climb monkey bars; watch your favorite funny movie; climb a tree; turn cartwheels across the lawn.

Remember... it isn't so much *what* you do as *how* you do it — and if it's done in a spirit of fun, you'll be rewarded with happiness in more ways than you can measure.

— *Avery Jakobs*

Let Go of Stress and Always Remember...

*Y*ou can't change the past and you can ruin a perfectly good present by worrying about the future.

— *Author Unknown*

*T*here is only one way to happiness and that is to cease worrying about things which are beyond the power of our will.

— *Epictetus*

...Everything Works Out for the Best

*A*lways expect the best. Then
if you have to hurdle a few tough
problems, you will have generated
the strength and courage to do so.

— George Matthew Adams

*H*ow great it is when we come to know
that times of disappointment can be followed
by times of fulfillment; that sorrow can be
followed by joy; that guilt over falling short
of our ideals can be replaced by pride in
doing all that we can; and that anger can be
channeled into creative achievements... and
into dreams that we can make come true!

— Fred Rogers

Even When
Skies Are Gray...

Everyone in life goes through a hard
time sometime, but you can't let that
define who you are. What defines you is
how you come back from those troubles
and what you find in life to smile about.

— *George Foreman*

Life is a journey through time,
filled with many choices; each of
us will experience life in our own
special way. So when days come
that are filled with frustration
and unexpected responsibilities,
remember to believe in yourself
and all you want your life to be.

— *Deanna Beisser*

...*Your Spirit Can Still Shine*

*E*veryone experiences loss. It comes with the joy of being human. What also comes with the package is our ability to prevail over any challenge and use our personal experiences for growth. There comes a point in each of our lives when we must realize that we are responsible for our own joy. Long-lasting happiness doesn't come from another person, your job, where you live, or how much money you make. We can make a conscious decision to have joy in our lives regardless of our situations.

— *Kathy Ireland and Laura Morton*

Discover What You Love to Do...

Finding happiness is like finding yourself. You don't find happiness, you make happiness. You choose happiness. Self-actualization is a process of discovering who you are, who you want to be, and paving the way to happiness by doing what brings YOU the most meaning and contentment to your life over the long run.

— *David Leonhardt*

Let each man find out what thing it is that nature specially intended him to do, and do it.

— *Archibald Lampman*

...and Then Pursue It

Simply seek happiness, and you are not
likely to find it. Seek to create and love
without regard to your happiness, and you
will likely be happy much of the time.

— *M. Scott Peck, MD*

If you want to reach out for happiness,
don't ever forget these words: you can
go as far as your dreams can take you.

— *Collin McCarty*

True Happiness
Lies Within

*T*he first step in finding happiness
is to stop relying on the outside
world to get us there — we need
to look deep into our own hearts
and souls to find the peace and
satisfaction that brings a shining
smile to our face.

— *Mary Lou Retton*

I think happiness comes from self-acceptance.
We all try different things, and we find some
comfortable sense of who we are. We look at
our parents and learn and grow and move on.
We change.

— *Jamie Lee Curtis*

$\mathcal{I}$'m learning that part of getting to know yourself is being able to look at your life as both an inner and an outer journey. I picture my outer journey as horizontal — I'm walking along and I can see the horizon, and all the familiar landmarks along the way. It is what I'm doing and where I'm going. My inner journey is vertical — with no horizon, no specific goal. In this journey, I'm taking one step at a time. I don't look backward or forward, but experience each moment. I am not doing — I am being.

The joy in the journey does not necessarily come from reaching a goal or from attaining the summit. Joy comes from what transpires along the way.

— *Lilias Folan*

$\mathcal{T}$o awake each morning with a smile brightening my face; to greet the day with reverence for the opportunities it contains; to approach my work with a clean mind; to meet men and women with laughter on my lips and love in my heart; to be gentle, kind, and courteous through all the hours; to approach the night with weariness that ever woos sleep and the joy that comes from work well done — this is how I desire to waste wisely my days.

— *Thomas Dekker*

A Happiness Affirmation

Happiness is an essential part of my life.
When I am happy, I feel incredibly alive.
I feel at peace with myself and with the
world. I try my best to find the lighter side
of every situation and surround myself
with people who keep my spirit inspired
and uplifted. I accept that there will be
times when darkness overcomes me. It's
okay for me to feel sad or angry sometimes.
These emotions are a healthy part of life,
but I will not allow them to linger long
enough to dim my light. Emotions are
contagious, and I will try my best to keep
those around me feeling glad.

— *Diane Mastromarino*

*H*appiness is not a thing, address, possession, bank balance, or life position (retirement, marriage, being single, parenthood, etc.). It is not something you can grasp, earn, keep, buy, learn, give away, or know. Happiness is not anything that you go after. It will come after you relentlessly if you have that inner state of consciousness that says, "I am happy no matter what is in my life."

This does not mean to imply that you will be happy 24 hours a day, 365 days a year. That would not be life as it was designed to be. It would also be exhausting! However, we were meant to be happy as a life destiny. Pain, grief, sadness, solitude, and, yes, even loneliness are all valuable contributors to a humble, joyous, compassionate, loving, balanced, and productive life.

You cannot totally experience the thrill of victory without ever tasting defeat. You cannot completely bask in the sunshine of success if you have never been brought to your knees. And you cannot know fully the joy of a happy disposition, spirit, and demeanor without ever knowing unhappiness.

Life is a wonderful adventure — filled with every imaginable emotion, experience, test, adversity, achievement, mistake, and success. Life is not, nor will it ever be, perfect. Life is not a dress rehearsal for some later event. Life is now; what is happening now, what you are experiencing now, what you are learning now, what you are doing now, what you are dreaming now, and what you are afraid of now.

— *Tim Connor*

Happiness Is All Around You

*H*appiness... can grow in any soil, live in any condition. It defies environment. It comes from within; it's the revelation of the depths of the inner life as light and heat proclaim the sun from which they radiate. Happiness consists not of having, but of being; not of possessing, but of enjoying. It is the warm glow of a heart at peace with itself.... Happiness is paradoxical because it may coexist with trial, sorrow, and poverty. It is the gladness of the heart, rising superior to all conditions.

— *William George Jordan*

$\mathcal{L}$ife is huge! Rejoice about the sun, moon, flowers, and sky. Rejoice about the food you have to eat. Rejoice about the body that houses your spirit. Rejoice about the fact that you can be a positive force in the world around you. Rejoice about the love that is around you. If you want to be happy, commit to making your life one of rejoicing.

— *Author Unknown*

What does it mean to be happy? Some call happiness a feeling of satisfaction, comfort, fulfillment, and inner peace. Others refer to joy, excitement, and communion. The sensation of happiness might be unique to each of us; however, we know when we're there. We can note certain common characteristics. When we are happy with ourselves, we are accepting of ourselves (not judging ourselves). When we are happy with others, we are accepting of them (not judging them). Happiness brings us closer together rather than pushing us apart. But above all, happiness makes love tangible.

— *Barry Neil Kaufman*

Have a Love Affair
with Life

When we're happy, we're living the life we're meant to live. We're being true to our inner nature, to who we really are. Our profound love of life is powerfully sustaining. Creating paradise on earth is having a love affair with life. Each hour, we can bring nearer to us more beauty, more loveliness, more things we value: a richer understanding of the reality of cause and effect, a growing library of good literature, a collection of life-enhancing paintings and drawings by favorite artists, an increasing knowledge about what ingredients go into a happy moment, a deeper appreciation for every breath of air we inhale and gratitude at being alive.

— Alexandra Stoddard

Secrets of
Lasting Happiness

One of the secrets of happiness is
to take time to accomplish what
you have to do, then to make time
to achieve what you want to do.

Remember that life is short. Its golden moments need hopes and memories and dreams. When it seems like those things are lost in the shuffle, you owe it to yourself to find them again. The days are too precious to let them slip away. If you're working too hard, make sure it's because it's a sacrifice for a time when you're going to pay yourself back with something more important than money could ever be. If you're losing the battle, do what it takes to win the war over who is in control of your destiny.

Find time, make time, take time… to do something rewarding and deeply personal and completely worthwhile. Time is your fortune, and you can spend it to bring more joy to yourself and to others your whole life through.

— *Douglas Pagels*

Think of the things that make you happy,
Not the things that make you sad;
Think of the fine and true in mankind,
Not its sordid side and bad;
Think of the blessings that surround you,
Not the ones that are denied;
Think of the virtues of your friendships,
Not the weak and faulty side;
Think of the hopes that lie before you,
Not the waste that lies behind;
Think of the treasures you have gathered,
Not the ones you've failed to find;
Think of the service you may render,
Not of serving self alone;
Think of the happiness of others,
And in this you'll find your own!

— *Robert E. Farley*

Find Happiness
in Everything You Do

Find happiness in nature
in the beauty of a mountain
in the serenity of the sea
Find happiness in friendship
in the fun of doing things together
in the sharing and understanding
Find happiness in your family
in the stability of knowing
   that someone cares
in the strength of love and honesty
Find happiness in yourself
in your mind and body
in your values and achievements
Find happiness in everything
you do

— *Susan Polis Schutz*

Let Happiness
Be Your Legacy

$\mathcal{T}$ry to make at least one person happy every day.... If you cannot do a kind deed, speak a kind word. If you cannot speak a kind word, think a kind thought. Count up, if you can, the treasure of happiness that you would dispense in a week, in a year, in a lifetime!

— Lawrence F. Lovasik

$\mathcal{E}$very heart that has beat strongly and cheerfully has left a hopeful impulse behind it in the world, and bettered the tradition of mankind.

— Robert Louis Stevenson

Don't Let Anything Steal Your Joy

Choose to be well in every way. Choose to be happy no matter what. Decide that each day will be good just because you're alive.

You have power over your thoughts and feelings. Don't let your circumstances dictate how you feel. Don't let your thoughts and feelings color your situation blue or desperate.

Even if you don't have everything you want, even if you're in pain or in need, you can choose to be joyful no matter what you're experiencing.

You are more than your body, your physical presence, and your material possessions. You are spirit. You have your mind, heart, and soul, and there is always something to be thankful for.

Decide that life is good and you are special. Decide to enjoy today. Decide that you will live life to the fullest now, no matter what. Trust that you will change what needs changing, but also decide that you're not going to put off enjoying life just because you don't have everything you want now. Steadfastly refuse to let anything steal your joy. Choose to be happy… and you will be!

— *Donna Fargo*

May You Find Happiness in Every Direction Your Paths Take You

May you never lose your sense of wonder, and may you hold on to the sense of humor you use to brighten the lives of everyone who knows you. May you go beyond the ordinary steps and discover extraordinary results. May you keep on trying to reach for your stars, and may you never forget how wonderful you are.

May you always be patient with the problems of life, and know that any clouds will eventually give way to the sunlight of your most hoped-for days. May you be rewarded with the type of friendships that get better and better — and the kind of love that blesses your life forever.

May you have enough material wealth to meet your needs, while never forgetting that the real treasures of life are the loved ones and friends who are invaluable to the end. May you search for serenity, and discover it was within you all along. May you know that you hold tomorrow within your hands, and that the way there will be shared with the makings of what will be your most wonderful memories. And may you always be happy, each step of the way.

— *R. L. Keith*

ACKNOWLEDGMENTS

We gratefully acknowledge the permission granted by the following authors, publishers, and authors' representatives to reprint poems or excerpts from their publications.

Barbara J. Hall for "Happiness is…." Copyright © 2008 by Barbara J. Hall. All rights reserved.

PrimaDonna Entertainment Corp. for "Ten Golden Rules for a Happy Life" and "Don't Let Anything Steal Your Joy" by Donna Fargo. Copyright © 2005, 2008 by PrimaDonna Entertainment Corp. All rights reserved.

Broadway Books, a division of Random House, Inc., for "Happy people are accepting…" from THE HAPPINESS MAKEOVER: HOW TO TEACH YOURSELF TO BE HAPPY AND ENJOY EVERY DAY by M. J. Ryan. Copyright © 2005 by M. J. Ryan. All rights reserved. And for "The first step in finding happiness…" from MARY LOU RETTON'S GATEWAY TO HAPPINESS by Mary Lou Retton. Copyright © 2000 by MLR Entertainment, Inc., and Momentum Partners, Inc. All rights reserved.

Viking Penguin, a division of Penguin Group (USA), Inc., for "A happy person is not someone to…" from HOW TO BE HAPPIER DAY BY DAY: A YEAR FULL OF MINDFUL ACTIONS by Alan Epstein, PhD. Copyright © 1993 by Alan Epstein. All rights reserved.

The Daily Motivator for "Start with Joy" by Ralph S. Marston, Jr. Copyright © 2007 by Ralph S. Marston, Jr. Used by permission. Originally published in *The Daily Motivator* at www.dailymotivator.com (December 7, 2007). All rights reserved.

Simon & Schuster Adult Publishing Group for "It isn't what you have…" from HOW TO WIN FRIENDS AND INFLUENCE PEOPLE by Dale Carnegie. Copyright © 1936 by Dale Carnegie, copyright renewed © 1964 by Donna Dale Carnegie and Dorothy Carnegie. Revised Edition copyright © 1981 by Donna Dale Carnegie and Dorothy Carnegie. All rights reserved. And for "Everyone in life goes…" from GEORGE FOREMAN'S GUIDE TO LIFE by George Foreman. Copyright © 2002 by George Foreman. All rights reserved.

Grand Central Publishing for "Gratitude is not precisely the same…" from LIGHTPOSTS FOR LIVING: THE ART OF CHOOSING A JOYFUL LIFE by Thomas Kinkade. Copyright © 1999 by Media Arts Group, Inc. Reprinted by permission of Grand Central Publishing. All rights reserved.

Rachel Snyder for "More than a feeling…." Copyright © 2008 by Rachel Snyder. All rights reserved.

Tribune Media Services for "For most of life…" from "In Happiness" by Andy Rooney. Copyright © 2002 by Andy Rooney. All rights reserved.

Condé Nast Publications for "I kept looking for happiness…" by Nicole Kidman from "The Lady Is Yar" by Krista Smith (*Vanity Fair*: October 2007). Copyright © 2007 by Condé Nast Publications. All rights reserved.

Earlnightingale.com for "Learn to enjoy every minute…" from THE STRANGEST SECRET by Earl Nightingale. Copyright © 1956 by Earl Nightingale. All rights reserved.

Delacorte Press, a division of Random House, Inc., for "We do not experience happiness…" from REAL MOMENTS by Barbara De Angelis, PhD. Copyright © 1994 by Barbara De Angelis. All rights reserved.

Michele Moore, www.happinesshabit.com, for "Happiness and Work" from HAPPINESS HABIT: SKILLS & STRATEGIES OF HABITUALLY HAPPY PEOPLE. Copyright © 2005 by Michele Moore. All rights reserved.

Michael Crichton for "If you want to be happy…" from "Happiness" (*Redbook*: May 1991). Copyright © 1991 by Michael Crichton. All rights reserved.

Crown Publishers, a division of Random House, Inc., for "Smile at someone…" from 365 WAYS TO CHANGE YOUR LIFE by Suzanne Somers. Copyright © 1999 by Suzanne Somers. All rights reserved.

Doubleday, a division of Random House, Inc., for "Everyone experiences loss" from POWERFUL INSPIRATIONS: EIGHT LESSONS THAT WILL CHANGE YOUR LIFE by Kathy Ireland and Laura Morton. Copyright © 2002 by Kathy Ireland WorldWide, Inc. All rights reserved.

David Leonhardt, www.thehappyguy.com, for "Finding happiness is like finding yourself" from "What is the definition of happiness, anyway?" Copyright © 2008 by David Leonhardt. All rights reserved.

Touchstone, a division of Simon & Schuster Adult Publishing Group, for "Simply seek happiness…" from THE DIFFERENT DRUM by M. Scott Peck, MD. Copyright © 1987 by M. Scott Peck, MD, PC. All rights reserved.

Reader's Digest for "I think happiness comes from…" by Jamie Lee Curtis from "Jamie Lee Curtis Interview: Starring as Herself " by Meg Grant (*Reader's Digest*: December 2004). Copyright © 2004 by *Reader's Digest*. All rights reserved.

Rodale Press for "I'm learning that part of getting…" from LILIAS! YOGA GETS BETTER WITH AGE by Lilias Folan. Copyright © 2005 by Lilias Folan. All rights reserved.

Tim Connor for "Happiness is not a thing…." From THAT'S LIFE!: 41 CHALLENGES AND HOW TO HANDLE THEM. Copyright © 2001 by Tim Connor. All rights reserved.

Fawcett Columbine, a division of Random House, Inc., for "What does it mean to be happy?" from HAPPINESS IS A CHOICE by Barry Neil Kaufman. Copyright © 1991 by Barry Neil Kaufman. All rights reserved.

HarperCollins Publishers for "Have a Love Affair with Life" from CHOOSING HAPPINESS: KEYS TO A JOYFUL LIFE by Alexandra Stoddard. Copyright © 2002 by Alexandra Stoddard. All rights reserved.

Sophia Institute Press for "Try to make at least…" from THE HIDDEN POWER OF KINDNESS by Lawrence G. Lovasik. Copyright © 1999 by Lawrence G. Lovasik. All rights reserved.

A careful effort has been made to trace the ownership of selections used in this anthology in order to obtain permission to reprint copyrighted material and give proper credit to the copyright owners. If any error or omission has occurred, it is completely inadvertent, and we would like to make corrections in future editions provided that written notification is made to the publisher:

BLUE MOUNTAIN ARTS, INC., P.O. Box 4549, Boulder, Colorado 80306.